"TODAY
I SEE THE
SUNRISE"

Daily Meditations for Survivors of Torture and Abuse

BY JULIE A. CIPOLLA

BALBOA.
PRESS
A DIVISION OF HAY HOUSE

Balboa Press books may be ordered through booksellers or by contacting:

Balboa Press
A Division of Hay House
1663 Liberty Drive
Bloomington, IN 47403
www.balboapress.com
1 (877) 407-4847

Because of the dynamic nature of the Internet, any web addresses or
links contained in this book may have changed since publication and
may no longer be valid. The views expressed in this work are solely those
of the author and do not necessarily reflect the views of the publisher,
and the publisher hereby disclaims any responsibility for them.

The author of this book does not dispense medical advice or prescribe the use
of any technique as a form of treatment for physical, emotional, or medical
problems without the advice of a physician, either directly or indirectly. The
intent of the author is only to offer information of a general nature to help
you in your quest for emotional and spiritual well-being. In the event you use
any of the information in this book for yourself, which is your constitutional
right, the author and the publisher assume no responsibility for your actions.

Any people depicted in stock imagery provided by Thinkstock are
models, and such images are being used for illustrative purposes only.
Certain stock imagery © Thinkstock.

Print information available on the last page.

ISBN: 978-1-5043-6735-6 (sc)
ISBN: 978-1-5043-6737-0 (hc)
ISBN: 978-1-5043-6736-3 (e)

Library of Congress Control Number: 2016916421

Balboa Press rev. date: 10/19/2016

JANUARY 1

Can I, a tortured soul, find glimpses of happiness?

If I end it all now, I'll never know if I'll meet those persons or that Person who brings joy, enlightenment, belief and restore me to my native self.

It takes more courage to live day by day with the burden of betrayal by other human beings we may have trusted. It takes more courage to live than to die at our own hands.

Can I now summon the courage to live just one more day?

For today, I will remember it takes more courage to live than to die – may I ask the Divine for that strength.

JANUARY 2

As a victim of torture, I wondered, why me? My helplessness, hopelessness and ugliness that I felt and was taught to believe about myself seemed to earn me more beatings, cruel insults and jibes.

What is my moral obligation – to myself and others?

To have compassion for the poor victim that I was; to feel sorrow for the pain I'd been put through needlessly, at the hands of my fellow human beings.

What hope can I glean from this experience? For sure, I will never hurt another creature as I've been tortured. I will feel compassion for all the helpless beings that inhabit the Earth, including that helpless part of myself. And, I will strive, through peaceful means, to make the world a more just place, calling to task the perpetrators of violence of every kind.

JANUARY 3

Can I live just a little closer to my true self – the joyous, carefree human I was meant to be before the betrayal occurred?

Does a good meal bring joy? Or, is it just an escape from the all-pervading pain of being betrayed by others, who were supposed to champion me; or at least respect me as a fellow human traveler – but did not. They either abused me cruelly or ignored and disrespected my needs altogether. How can I recover from such a plight?

Seize moments day by day, with snippets of joy, peace, absolution for the helpless ones we were.

JANUARY 4

Today I am whole, though I was not when my abuser was busy at my soul murder. I have survived for a reason – to carry out a sacred mission on Earth. Of this I must be sure – else God would not have spared me.

Today I will remember that God loves me no matter the incomplete state I am in, nor the injured, nor damaged self I may carry. I am a precious piece of God's Love – a joy never to be repeated again. And as such, I will not focus on my faults and imperfections; only the fact that I am – perfect as I am.

JANUARY 5

Today, I seek to be whole, though it may be hard for me to find a normalcy after what was done to me. I will search for happiness for it is truly my birthright, as it is for every creature on Earth. I hope to find the joy in you and in me, that my victimizers cannot take away from me.

My abusers may have taken away my health, my sanity and my financial well-being; but my abusers cannot take away my soul's purity, goodness, and ability to Love.

Today I will remember that joy is my soul's birthright, and I will ever strive to be happy.

JANUARY 6

How do I feel about my being hurt? I feel alone, scared, sad and angry. I have been "tenderized" by my experiences. Some people become "tougher" and callous towards others. Never let me forget what it is to suffer and dear God do not let me hurt another intentionally or unintentionally.

I pray for Divine help with my tenderizing experiences – let them make me a deeper, better, more compassionate person – and never let me forget that others have feelings.

JANUARY 7

Today I feel the sunshine. Today I feel the rain. Today, I feel . . . .

When I was being tortured and abused, I could feel nothing. Everything felt unreal. Everything feeling unreal is a natural reaction to being abused. It was my escape from the pain of being betrayed, by those I trusted.

I hope to capture today's beauty – just for today. I hope to feel the day's joy – just for today. I hope to bask in the sunlight of God's Love for me and for everyone.

JANUARY 8

Today, I see the sunrise, in all its glory. Today I see myself in all my glory. I have survived great hardship. I have survived partly because of my own inner strength; and partly because of Divine intervention.

I hope to achieve my goals in the sunshine of a day free from abuse and torture. I hope to help another soul on its journey to freedom, from guilt, shame, loneliness or despair.

Just for today, I will remember I have been given the inner resources to survive abuse and torture and to reach a new day.

JANUARY 9

Today I will remember that I am not free from the trauma of abuse and torture, until I embrace myself in all my human vulnerability. My need for respect was trampled on. But I must remember that not all people are like that. I have the power to be kind to myself and to others. As long as I have the ability to love, my soul is not lost.

Today I will remember that having given love to unworthy others, it is not really lost – it comes back to me in multiples, via the Divine.

JANUARY 10

Today is the day I will try my best to recover from what abuse and torture, at others' hands has done to me. I will consciously seek joy and contemplation.

Today is a day when I can try my best to be joyful and kind to myself. Especially, I will make the effort to do for myself those things which make me happy, even if it means a little extra effort on my part. I deserve happiness, peace, joy, friendship and Love.

JANUARY 11

Today is the first day of the rest of my life. Although memories and flashbacks of the torture I experienced haunt me, they cannot hurt me now. They are rather old reminders of where I once was. I am free today, and even though I have these memories – they cannot really hurt me, now.

Today, I can build *new* memories, as I learn to love myself, and with precious others whom I love and who love me in return.

JANUARY 12

Today I will remember that I am *not* all alone. I have my magnificent self – my surviving self – filled with Divine sparkle and energy. I can reach out to others who have suffered as I have, to give and receive love and support; and to learn how to love myself.

I reach towards the Divine, and am assured of God's kind Love sent to me at just the times when I need it the most.

Today, I will remember that I am not alone. Instead, I'm part of a community of souls who reach towards Divine peace and serenity.

JANUARY 13

Today is the day I *will* myself to be alive. It is a day in which I am lucky to be alive. I may not always feel so lucky, because the memories of the pain of being abused are still so present in my heart. But if I remember that others also suffer at the hands of fellow human beings – I can reach out to help others create a more just and peaceful world.

Let me not make the mistake of harming another, just because I am in pain or angry or sad because I was tortured and abused. I believe that the Divine asks me to forgive, so I can heal and be at peace, permanently.

JANUARY 14

Today I recognize that I am loved. Even though I sometimes feel shame, pain and loneliness, I know I am loved. I realize that I am worthy, though I may not always feel worthy.

I am worthy of love, because I am a Divine Soul with a purpose and a journey, which does not end with this life, nor with the abuse. My soul's journey is infinite and it is guided by God – the God of my own understanding.

JANUARY 15

I have a memory of happiness. How ever dim the memory of joy is, I will meditate on it. I will commune with the Divine, and put myself in a place where I can most soak in the sunshine rays of Divine tenderness.

I was once a tortured soul. Indeed I am Holy – a product of God's creation. I did not deserve the abuse I went through. Instead I deserved then and I deserve now, the Love and compassion of God, myself and my fellow travelers.

JANUARY 16

Today is the day I am alive, for better or for worse. I will gently face the pain of having been abused and tortured at the hands of fellow human beings. Yes I am alive!

I will practice gentleness and kindness with myself, though I was taught to feel shame and self hatred. I will practice loving myself. Every day that goes by, will find my love for myself growing, as well as my admiration for myself and my ability to survive and thrive despite the experience of torture.

Today I will remember that I am worthy of love and tenderness, especially because I went through so much.

JANUARY 17

Today holds the totality of all the wisdom of my life – what I've experienced before this and today, including the abuse and torture. I hope that I will remember that I am loveable. This I say to my abusers: "I am God's Child, and your cruelty cannot touch my Divinity, nor my ability to Love.

Today I will remember that the Divine spark that is me, is alive with joy and relief at being freed at last from torture and abuse.

JANUARY 18

Today I will remember that I am loveable no matter how ugly or unlovable my torturers wanted me to believe I was. I am a Divine spark and as such, I have a lot to offer myself and to the world.

I am lovable even though I may feel ashamed of how helpless I was at the hands of my abusers.

Today is the day I will rejoice in my own goodness and power for good as a human being.

JANUARY 19

Praise God that I have survived my torturer's abuse of me. It is not through my own strength alone, but Divine strength given to me by God to survive the ordeals I have come through.

God's loving kindness has preserved me, so that I may fulfill His Divine purpose – His Plan – Love in this world.

I am alive and awake because of Him, not through the mirage of my own faltering strength. And so I praise Him.

JANUARY 20

I have received a gift from God – my life restored to me after the ordeals of torture.

I hardly know how to claim it – hardly know who I am now – but if I pray, I will find not only the truth about who I am, but I will find a Person in God, whom I may rely on.

Abuse often leaves us without an identity, generating a lonely, empty feeling. Just accepting myself in all my aspects will awaken my true identity – a Child of God, Who is a loving Parent.

JANUARY 21

I remember a soulless, wandering time – when my abusers were all around me – and there was no one to witness the physical torture and emotional torment I went through. There was no one to validate that I was *not* crazy, when I described those incidents of overt or covert betrayal, when my torturers tried to hide behind a veil of decency.

I remember a time when I had no one to look to but God, who witnessed all that was being done to me. I felt all alone and crazy, for realizing that those I loved and trusted would hurt me, by acts of violence or acts of neglect in not protecting me – in permitting it to go on.

Now I have witnesses; other torture survivors, therapists, friends or family members who have the courage to speak up and say the immorality of what was and is still being done to others in the world.

JANUARY 22

I remember a time when I couldn't speak, couldn't pray – I was in so much pain, and did not know if I would live through it, nor knew if I wanted to.

But I have God as my deliverer from the horrors of torture and betrayal – my champion. I have been kept alive for some Divine purpose, and whatever that turns out to be, I embrace that purpose with all my being, and all my doing.

I have heard God, as a whisper telling me that I shall live – though it may take courage to deal with all those flashbacks and sleepless nights. I can be a witness to my brother's or sister's pain, and a witness to them that through God's help, we shall all have brighter, better days.

JANUARY 23

I hope for a better tomorrow, though my tortured days were so dark and tinged with pain and sadness. I will remember that there is such a thing as joy, as levity. I must actively seek the joy-filled aspects of life, as I let go of the pain of the abuse.

I will retrain my mind to anticipate pleasure and joy, Love and repose. And I will train my heart to seek out injustice wherever it is on Earth and not to close my eyes to anyone's suffering.

JANUARY 24

I will hope, for today. Let today be the day when I find a glimmer of joy, and decency in others. I know I can rely on my God not to let me down. But what about my brothers and sisters in life? Will I look for the good in others, or have I become jaded by my experiences of being abused that I no longer feel capable of seeing the good in anybody?

Perhaps I will look to myself and others, as manifestations of the Divine spark, as testimony to the goodness of God.

JANUARY 25

Today I will pray for inspiration to carry out my daily duties, especially those for myself. I am a valuable person, regardless of what my abusers would have had me believe.

I am a Child of God, a creation wholly unique and special; a one-of-a-kind, who never will be created again. I have a destiny that is Divinely-given.

JANUARY 26

Can you remember the day you were liberated from the camp of your torturers? I remember the day I was set free.

The night felt so peaceful, no longer to be beaten or ridiculed – just to have Peace. It was God who granted me this day, when so many did not make it.

Let us whisper our thanks, and may our lives honor those who did not make it.

JANUARY 27

Today I see the sunrise . . . . Today I feel the rain. I am alive. I am free. Flashbacks and sleepless nights make my freedom seem conditional. But I awaken to embrace the day. I embrace all the possibilities of this day, for I am *fully alive* to embrace God's will for my life.

JANUARY 28

I cannot remember a time when there was no pain. I must actively search out the joys and levity of life, else life seems unbearable. It is my job to search for the fun, happy and joyous moments. I must actively seek out the moments of connection with myself, and with other human beings and other creatures too, who bring meaning and purpose to my life.

JANUARY 29

I can remember the sunshine in my day; the blue skies in the midst of pain. Walking on the sunny side of the street, I don't deny the pain of the torture I've experienced. However, I choose to embrace the current moment as a moment of peace, free from abuse. I need to embrace friendships with those other human beings, as by their kindnesses and love, will heal my pain – perhaps other survivors, or other warm human beings and creatures, as God may choose to put into my life.

JANUARY 30

I feel the pain of loneliness. Perhaps others do not understand the torture and abuse I've been put through and its consequent shame. But I am a creature of God, a child of the Creator, unique and special, whole and beloved. I do not need my abusers' permission to exist; they do not give me life; it is by my Creator's Hand that I live and move and have my being.

JANUARY 31

It is by the Creator's hand that I live and exist, move and am. I do not need the permission of my torturers and abusers to have a life. My life is what I make of it. I may have flashbacks; I may have pain or shame. But I can counter them with thoughts of those who love me now, and my relationships today with caring people – and the Divine.

FEBRUARY 1

I hope you have me for a friend, for I will not betray you. I have been tortured and abused by those I was supposed to trust, and perhaps so have you. In any case, we see examples all around us of the inhuman acts perpetrated by people on others, such as ethnic cleansing. We know that such behavior is completely contrary to what the Creator has intended for us.

Today I will remember that kindness seeps into all the squeaky places to silence the pain of betrayal; kindness seeps into all the rough places to make them smooth and receptive to Love.

FEBRUARY 2

I remember the horror of the abuse in my life and have compassion for myself, knowing that I am a Child of God. I was not deserving of the filthy things that were done to me, no matter how much those in power said or acted as if I was. I am a Child of God, and as such, am fit to do His work, and to receive His comfort and Love in my Heart.

Today I will remember God's love for me – that I am so much more than simply a survivor of abuse and torture. I am a Divine Soul with much to offer myself and the world around me.

FEBRUARY 3

I will remember the torture all of my life. I will also remember that my life is worth so much more than I was taught to believe, for I am precious Soul. I identify with all the victims of war, racism, sexual violence, and every other kind of cruelty. Each of us is a Divine Soul with a worth and existence beyond what is ordinarily revealed in this world.

Let me open my heart to survivors of torture and abuse, starting with myself.

FEBRUARY 4

Today I see the sun of triumph over the beatings, burnings, sexual molestations and verbal abuse – all brands of soul murder. I am regaining my soul, in bits and pieces, but my soul *is* coming back to me. I am becoming the self that I was meant to be, had the torture and abuse not occurred. In fact, I am a better, more compassionate and loving person because of it.

FEBRUARY 5

This is a new day, and I am alive, due to the Divine Plan. I may wonder how I'll have the courage to embrace the day, with its share of heartaches, as well as its joys. This is so, especially as I am a trauma survivor, and most especially since that trauma was caused by the cruelty or thoughtlessness of other human beings.

I will have the courage today to open my eyes and heart to this day. I will trust in my God that I am an essential thread of His Divine Plan woven into Life's fabric.

FEBRUARY 6

Have you heard a song that lifts your spirits? Today I will listen for a song with special meaning. I will try to savor its deeper spiritual significance – for I can hear God's message of loving acceptance in a song. Let me sing that song to other survivors to soothe them and together we will create more Hope for the world.

FEBRUARY 7

Today I heard a word that gave me encouragement. It was a word that helped me glimpse how precious I am, to myself, to the world, and to God. I am at my most creative when I feel I have something higher to offer. My torturers wanted me to believe that I have nothing of value to offer, and that I did not even deserve to live. They wanted me to believe I deserved all the pain. It's been a long journey since, with more worthwhile people, who have helped me to believe that I am a valuable human being.

FEBRUARY 8

I may feel betrayed by my helpless self which couldn't protect me from the abuse, because the tormenters were too strong. It's just what my torturers wanted me to believe – that I was at fault, somehow, for the abuse they perpetrated on me. They did not take responsibility for their own cruel actions. I used to feel responsible, if only to hold onto some semblance of control, which of course, I had none at the time of the abuse.

FEBRUARY 9

I'd like to learn to love my helpless self, instead of scorn, or hate this part of myself. How do I learn to love my vulnerable humanness? By smiling at myself in the mirror; holding myself when I need soothing; surrounding myself with caring, loving people and surrendering to the loving kindness of God's healing power.

FEBRUARY 10

Today is the day that I see the sunrise through the wintry sky. My life is like that too – I can see beauty in the midst of pain. Though I hope for less pain and more joy, life has its share of both.

Today, let me remember to be kind to myself amidst the pain and the joy of life. Let me feel the kindness of my soul, so readily given to others. Let me feel the joy of loving myself.

FEBRUARY 11

Today is the day I will arise with the dawn and greet the day. I will comb my hair and do my grooming so I will feel loved. My body is important, not just what I think or feel, or believe or hope or dream.

Today I will remember that good grooming, especially when I look my best, can make me feel on top of the world.

FEBRUARY 12

I hope I can find you among the flowers at dawn; or perhaps in the glory of the night with the moon and the stars.

I hope we see and acknowledge each other; as I await the next revelation of God's will for me.

Now is the time for us to arise and do things worthy of our natures, of our souls – Whether it is to sing, or to dance or to sculpt or to joyfully serve ourselves, God and each other.

FEBRUARY 13

Now is the time for us to arise to do those things which our natures call us to do – to love, to dream, to believe and to lie basking in the glow of God's Love.

I hope we will find each other among the flowers today. We were tortured, but we can have good days or parts of good days, even if they are mere moments.

Let's savor those moments when we can feel peace and even joy. And then let's spread this joy to others who need a helping hand. It will help us to feel deep purpose and meaning in our lives.

FEBRUARY 14

If I feel the sly sleeping-sickness, which is really depression trying to overtake me; I will take on a Martial arts spirit, to keep me in touch with my primal energy.

I will use the discipline of the martial arts to express the primal urge to be alive and active in life. I will not let depression overtake me, for I am too valuable to God and to this world. I can do it no good if I am sleeping my life away or vegging out on TV or some other mindless, numbing activity.

FEBRUARY 15

Today, like me, I hope you will find that it takes two to argue. So I will not argue today, but agree to disagree, for my soul's serenity is too precious.

Let's count aloud as we practice punches or kicks into the air, but do no harm to ourselves or to others. Instead let our primal energy bring about a more just society.

FEBRUARY 16

Today I will focus on the *fact* that though I have been tortured, I have much to live for; to help myself and others to reach our potentials. We are so powerful and wonderful! Let's not let the torture take that reality from our sight!

I will remember the wonderful beauty of my soul and of yours, too.

FEBRUARY 17

Let us watch the sunrise together. Tortured and wounded though we may be; we *are alive* to tell our stories of how we were graced by God to survive such hardships.

In the dawn, we see a bright new day, though our pain may be great, our loneliness acute, our sadness plentiful. "You are not alone, for I am with you," says the All-Loving Presence.

FEBRUARY 18

Today, I have a choice: I can sulk and sink deeper into depression, or I can arise, have a good breakfast and begin the day full of my soul's purpose and love.

Ecstasy is not always possible – but I can feel fulfilled in that I have searched out my soul's purpose and found how I can be useful and helpful to myself and to others.

Perhaps it's just giving a smile or friendly greeting – but I am *alive* today to give it. Perhaps it's just a reassuring touch, but I am alive to give it, or receive it, which I am not, if I hibernate in my bed.

FEBRUARY 19

I'm reminded of a time when I wasn't so alive. It was in the midst of my torture. I couldn't state my soul's Purpose, because my very survival was at stake. I had to be so mute – that my soul's longing was hidden even from myself.

I was not at fault; my first priority (and rightly so) was to survive. When terror was rained down upon me with blows to my body and soul, I could not think of the future. I only thought to survive. I had to numb myself to my true Purpose.

Today I no longer need to numb my primal energy. I can rejoice in it, now that I have survived, by the Grace of God.

FEBRUARY 20

I hope you will remember a time when you were alone as a time when God held your hand, as He did mine; even as I felt alone.

I hope you will remember a time when you felt alone and now you no longer have to feel so isolated, for we are of the community of human beings who have experienced something extraordinary. By the Grace of God we survived with our souls intact. It may not feel as if our souls are intact, because those soul murderers who tortured us and made us feel terror and self loathing, almost won out. But God has intervened and helped us to regain our belief in our own God-given worth.

FEBRUARY 21

Understand that it's not what we do in life but the fact of our giving of ourselves. I must remember to be gentle first with myself and then with others, especially those who have been tortured as I once was. I can feel alive with pleasure and now I wish to spread that joy to all creatures.

For those of us who were raised in childhood terror of one or more guardians, that joy and spontaneity may be hard to come by. But rest assured, our soul's urge is to be joyous and free. It will naturally rise to the surface, as the torture passes from our daily reality to just a memory.

FEBRUARY 22

Today I begin the rest of my life. I remember harshness and brutality heaped upon me, which is instructive of how I must never be. Gentle and kind must I be, because I know how it hurts to be wounded and ignored.

FEBRUARY 23

I am inspired to sing the praises of a God who allowed me to survive the pain of abuse. I was angry with Him for letting me undergo such painful attacks but I realized that what I endured was contrary to His all-Loving Will. People who are cruel have free will, so there are no guarantees. Just as I have free will to do good things or to hurt others, those who tortured me had a free choice and they chose to harm me. I must remember my own free will and exercise good judgment and compassion in its use.

FEBRUARY 24

Today I accept God's Love in all its forms. I accept with grace all the good that comes my way.

It seemed the only power I had, was when I gave love so it became hard to receive love, because I was no longer in control of the gift nor the giver.

Today I will remember that it was not on my own that I survived the torture and the abuse; and I will not make it through this life without the kindness and love of others and of God.

FEBRUARY 25

Today I feel liberated from pain, if even only for a moment or two. I am alive and I have purpose – my existence has meaning for myself and for others.

Today I will remember my purpose, even as a broken being due to the torture – I can still do God's will.

FEBRUARY 26

Once I cried inconsolably. Who knew then that I would reach this day of victory over my oppressors? My God is at my side. My heart beats aloud for I have conquered, by the Grace of God, and the love of other human beings.

FEBRUARY 27

I will find peace of mind in giving love and in receiving love from my fellow creatures and my God.

I may forgive my torturers so I will have peace of mind. Though I may forgive I must never forget the dangers of cruelty and selfishness.

FEBRUARY 28

I recall a time when I was sad. It seemed the whole world was coming to an end. I never envisioned feeling joy again. But the day of joy has come, and I'm lifting my head a little from the ground where my attackers left me. I can see the sunrise, and that I have a purpose just as does the Sun and Moon and all creatures on Earth.

FEBRUARY 29

I have a new friend – me. I can be good to myself even though I was taught to hate myself, by those who hurt me. They took me at my weakest, most vulnerable point and nearly crushed my soul; so that I thought that joy was only for others, but not for me.

Today, I know that I deserve to feel joy; to feel Life, to feel the Love of God and my fellows within me.

MARCH 1

Today I feel the sunshine, though it is an early spring day. I can glory in my own existence as well as in others'. I can live free, though I may have flashbacks and memories of the abuse. I can live free, thanks to God's Grace.

I hope you will remember there is another side to existence – a joyful one, even if only for a minute or two. Raise your head and see the sunrise and feel its warmth, and see the clouds parting to let the dawn start the new day.

MARCH 2

Today is the first day of the rest of my life. I can choose to live it in boredom and depression, or with interest in people and projects which I can complete, if I only have faith in God and myself.

Those who tortured us, tried to destroy our creativity, because that was the truest mark of our souls. Let us remember to be creative today, if only in the small choices we may make.

MARCH 3

I see you there, my Friend! For so many years, I was invisible – my needs counted for nothing. My torturers would have me believe that I didn't count, because they had continually denied me my humanity. My basic needs were denied, and so I came to believe that I didn't matter.

But I am God's Child, a creature no less than the sun, the clouds and the birds, with an awesome beauty as much as these.

Today I will remember to pray and thank God for the awesomeness of my existence.

MARCH 4

This is the day God has created – with me in it. My abusers never wanted me to have any future that was free of their governance and control.

But now I am free – free to live as I wish, even if I'm not so sure what shape that life will take.

I will remember, above all to be true to myself, my desires and dreams and wishes and hopes for the future.

MARCH 5

I will remember to rise in the morning with that martial arts spirit – for I have been a victim of torture and abuse. I often must fight to secure my right to live and exist in this world. Let me have a martial arts spirit, that rises above all abuse and establishes me firmly in the Heart of God.

MARCH 6

Today I will remember to be honest with myself about the pain I endured through their abuse, no matter how subtle. I will remember to honor the survival of my soul, just as now I will honor the joy I feel at being free at last.

Today I will remember that honesty is the best policy with regard to matters of my soul.

MARCH 7

Today I will remember to hold the hands of others who have suffered torture and cruelty at human whim. I will not let my brothers and sisters walk alone – just as I need them, to help me to remember my humanity.

We will walk together and reclaim our souls and our futures, into the bright new dawn, that was prepared for us.

MARCH 8

I can remember a time when I was too sad to think of hope. I just wanted to die, so that the pain of abuse and humiliation would end.

But I see a new day today – I've lived to tell about it. I'm now beyond the torturers' clutches; and though memories may humiliate me again – I know the abuser's behavior was not my fault in any way, shape or form.

MARCH 9

Today I see the sunrise – a new day shines before me. I'm alive!
I am at last free of the clutches of those who had abused me.
I may feel totally alone – but I'm never alone with You dear
God, beside me.

I am alive; by Your Grace and constant watching over me. May
I serve Your loving purpose on this Earth – as a beacon to those
still lost and floundering in their days of torture and abuse.

MARCH 10

I have heard a story of healing and of peace. It is *my* story. I have survived horrific torture at the hands of those who abused their power over me. But God, who is more powerful and loving than any human, has seen fit to save me.

I may have flashbacks – they are just old companions – they cannot hurt me as my abusers once did.

Today I will strive to live a peaceful life; one filled with inspiration and love, to give to my brothers and sisters on their journey with me.

MARCH 11

I have heard your sigh; I have felt your pain. You are not alone. We belong to a community of people who has learned first-hand the meaning of cruelty, at other human beings' hands. Rather than being bitter, we strive to avoid the mistakes of our torturers, and instead to embrace love, serving one another and God.

MARCH 12

I hope you will remember the value of your life, and not take it away, because you feel devastated as I once did. We can survive the abuse that our torturers heaped upon us.

If I die today I will not see the sunshine of the morning; nor feel the embrace of Someone who is in my life with unconditional Love.

Today – Let me remember the value of my life.

MARCH 13

If I torture myself with what I might have done to stop the abuse, I will miss the *utter innocence* of my soul.

I, like so many others who have been through genocide, wars, child abuse, rape, domestic violence, slavery, economic abuse, or other attacks, am a victim of others' cruelty. I had no part in contributing to it; and as such my one job has been to survive to a better day.

MARCH 14

Today I see your tears; as mine once used to be – relentless in their torrents. The sadness and aloneness seem unending to you now. But time is a true Healer allowing the finer details of our torture to fade and disappear into nothingness.

God grant us hope and peace and yes, joy.

MARCH 15

Today I see the sunshine – yesterday, I couldn't. The pain of having been relentlessly tortured by those I trusted to protect me, was too much. I wanted to die; but now I want to live – to jump and shout that I am alive.

Today I will remember to be gentle with my fellows, who may not feel like jumping for joy, just yet.

MARCH 16

Today I wipe your tears for the memories have been too much for you. You are not alone . . . as I am not alone. The Almighty has seen fit to let us survive horrific times – to survive for His loving purposes.

May we discover and celebrate this Purpose and live enriched by it.

MARCH 17

Now I see the sunrise for what it is – a manifestation of God's glory as *I* am a manifestation of that glory. No matter how battered and lost I may be, I am still God's Child, and as such, warmed by His love.

I feel God's tenderness seep into me like the sunshine into my skin. May I no more remember the horrors of my torture – but look ahead to Glory.

MARCH 18

I look into His glory and see the sunshine on the land. I have witnessed horror and pain, beyond human enduring. Yet, today is a new day – a day filled with promise and yes, maybe even with hope.

I hope you will join me; you who were battered both physically and spiritually—join me to see the day unfold, entrusted to His care.

MARCH 19

I am alive by the Grace of God – and now I must fulfill His purpose – no matter how lost I may feel. I ask for direction and guidance and know that though I may be battered, I am not absolved from seeking His will and meaning for my life.

I may have been damaged at the hands of cruel human beings; but today, I must find meaning for my life.

MARCH 20

I looked up and saw my God descending to reach me and end my torture so as I could begin life anew. I was so weak I could barely reach to my God, so my Creator covered most of the distance between us.

No word from the Almighty was spoken, but joy was His presence and Peace was His countenance. I am strengthened by His kindness. I am alive!

MARCH 21

This is a new day dawning – awakening. When I suffered I did not want to greet the day – I wanted only to die – to end my unbearable suffering.

I have survived to this point and so have you, my Friend. Let us break the cycle of abuse and be ushered unto a new day filled with peace, joy, purpose and meaning.

MARCH 22

Glory in today: we have surpassed the horrors of abuse and torture. In a way these horrors are always a part of us; but there is another side to life – the joy of our voices singing gratitude to God.

We may feel so beaten down, we ask, "How can we lift up our heads in praise?" Perhaps if we just lift up our eyes, God will do the rest.

MARCH 23

As deep as was my despair when I was under the power of those who would hurt me, as exultant is my joy, for though I do not forget what was done to me, I have lived to see another day.

MARCH 24

In the depths of despair, I see God's tears in the morning dew as the sun breaks through at dawn. My hope is renewed and so can yours be. . . . We can fight another day for our right to experience joy, peace, serenity. And, perhaps to forgive those who harmed us, so that our own hearts will heal.

We do not have to have a relationship with our perpetrators: yet we can forgive when we are ready. The harm that was done is lasting; yet so are our immortal souls; cleansed with *letting go of need for revenge.*

MARCH 25

Today I see the sunrise and the deer. The creatures of the night disappear into the hustle and bustle of a new day. My soul is stretched, reaching for the new challenges and blessings of the day.

If I've learned one thing, it is to err on the side of compassion; to lower my expectations of myself and all others and to just "be," while allowing others to "just be."

MARCH 26

I arise with the light and feel worry that is too much to bear. I may have been triggered by a bad dream or some other bad memory.

I only have to turn to God and trust His all-encompassing, soothing Love for me. God's "in my corner." He knows just what will bring me joy and fulfillment; such as helping another person, expressing myself and having a warm repose at the end of the day.

MARCH 27

Love is a broken emotion for many of us – fraught with pain, misunderstanding, and betrayal – so how can we trust *one more time?* How do we get up one more time to try again to love ourselves, others and God?

It starts by closing our eyes, spreading our arms out like a soaring eagle and surrendering to the overwhelming joy that God's love and kindness bring.

MARCH 28

We can be examples of self-control instead of lashing out at anyone (or ourselves), because we were hurt by someone. We restrain ourselves and retrain ourselves to have hope in better things. Then we can welcome goodness and abundance when, through God's intervention, the joys of Life finally do come.

MARCH 29

Self-love is not a sin; it is a necessity for our Soul's survival; for our ultimate achievement of fulfillment, and happiness.

Let us look to God as the model, for as the Divine loves us, so can we learn to love ourselves. Even if the abuse made us feel unworthy of love, or "dirty" or "evil," we are each God's Perfect Creation. We are a ray of sun in God's Heart, and entirely worthy of Love.

MARCH 30

It is a Mystery why we were created, why we were hurt, and how we came out of it as whole human beings.

It matters not what was done to us, by hurting, desperate, angry and frustrated human beings, or those with wonton disregard for our humanity. What matters is, do we retain our own humanity, our ability to love, regardless of the flashbacks, the physical and nervous sensations and body memories?

MARCH 31

Now is our time to shine for:

"What is to give light must endure burning." Viktor Frankl

Either we are still enduring horrific abuse; or, our time for deliverance has come. For some, deliverance comes too late and peace exists only in death. I mourn for my brother and sister Innocents who perished without a moment of joy or reprieve from their abusers.

APRIL 1

Is it possible to have compassion for those who harmed us? If we have not lost our humanity, we can see the pain and desperation of our brother and sister persecutors. For others who have no conscience and have harmed us, we can love whatever remains that is human about them, while seeking protection under the Angels' mighty wings.

APRIL 2

I am safe at last – and yet not all of us will make it. This is why we must reach out our hands and hearts to those who still suffer, remembering to identify ourselves as fellow travelers and therefore worthy of Love.

APRIL 3

Like the Spring, Hope is eternal. When we feel most alone, that is when God and the Angels are poised to help us to come back to ourselves. Let us not forget the legacy of the painful past, lest we repeat it by harming others, or devaluing ourselves.

APRIL 4

When it's our time to die, will we remember our past with pain, or peace? The time of death is near for some of us. At this time, let us remember just how Precious we are, for we are a *piece of God*, and bring joy to His Heart.

APRIL 5

When we were traumatized, we bargained with God, begging for the abuse to be over. For some of us, it was over, but not at a time of our choosing. We felt helpless and hopeless, alone and worthless. Yet the lies the abusers told us, could never stand up to the Light of God's Magnificent Grace. We are being hugged by God's warming love for us.

APRIL 6

Our soul is a Godly spark, just waiting to join with other Divine sparks and with God. No one can obliterate our Divine worth, no matter how hard they may try. We can all join together to forgive our abusers, and to forgive ourselves.

APRIL 7

Have no fear – our God is near – cradling us warmly, embracing us gently, and snugly in Her arms. No one can interfere with the Divine Love. We are worthy, even though we were beaten, tortured, sexually abused and psychologically and spiritually tormented. We know at last that we are worthy of being Loved.

APRIL 8

The nature of our Being, is such that when horrific acts of unkindness and cruelty take place, we ask, why? What have *I* done to deserve this? Children, especially, ask this; but so do all victims.

There is no "rhyme or reason" it seems. Yet if we honor ourselves, we will realize that the question is irrelevant, for the acts perpetrated on us were *not our misdeeds.* We may have contributed to the dynamics of abuse (or not), yet we are not responsible for it. The perpetrators decided on their own to do these unspeakable acts.

APRIL 9

We said something that "ticked him off," or we did something to "push her buttons." Perhaps our acts were infuriating to the other. And if so, as rational adults, a closer look at our behavior is required. Still, the abuser's violent response *is always and categorically wrong* and something which *they* need to look at. We are *not* responsible for the choices of our abusers, only our own.

APRIL 10

Can we compare our suffering to the countless brother and sister Beings on Earth who suffer? We can join our sufferings with theirs, and seek all together to relieve the suffering of the world. For only one who has suffered deeply can know what it means, and therefore be moved with compassion to help fellow beings.

And this is our legacy: cruelty to suffering – suffering to compassion – compassion to Love.

APRIL 11

It is our time to be concerned with the welfare of the world. Through compassion, we can supply the caring that is lacking. After we've turned to love ourselves, first, we can love each other, never again allowing abuse and cruelty to exist in the world.

Our abusers are part of the world. Let us turn towards them and thank them for teaching us compassion.

APRIL 12

Let's remember when we felt so lonely and worthless, and shut off from any kind of help. We may have felt that God had abandoned us, or even that God had permitted this suffering. The pain *is real*. Yet, … it is a mirage, compared with the comfort of God's Love for us.

APRIL 13

Experiencing compassion for the first time; breathing in that fragrance of caring, draws us out of ourselves with humility. We are all fragrant blossoms of God's Tree, and as such, with all the Beings of the universe, we are deserving of love and respect.

APRIL 14

When in doubt, respond with compassion and restraint, gentleness, understanding, tenderness and love towards *all*. When we see the mounting tension in others, we can reduce the strain with a smile, which costs nothing, and offers understanding relief for a hurting heart.

APRIL 15

How is it that when we acknowledge another's person's Divinity, we cannot help but see the divinity of our own souls? That divinity may have been obscured, especially the divinity of our perpetrators, who have hurt us so much. But our eyes can be opened to their Divinity with the vision of compassion.

APRIL 16

How can I remember good times if I've never had them? Always strife, pain, slaving, disappointment, alienation and loneliness have been my lot.

Yet, I have seen colors of blue (for the sky) and red for the sun as it sets. I know a larger Mind is at work – a Loving Heart that brings these sights to my eyes, just at the moment when I most need to see and feel them. Could God be saying "Hang in there, Kid, I love you?"

APRIL 17

I have seen glorious vistas. I have witnessed the Universe spinning in perfect synchronization with God's Plan. Could my life also be in synchronous orbit, a perfect ballet of Love, ordained by the Master?

APRIL 18

It could look to an outsider like my life is in chaos: no money, or, plenty of money and no peace. Or I may have an illness and pain that occupy all my time. Let not my abusers convince me that my life is worthless: I am learning from these trials to have compassion for myself and the next suffering traveler.

APRIL 19

Spring in the Northern Hemisphere brings autumn in the Southern Hemisphere. So, too, our lives are balanced, sometimes happy and sometimes sad. Good things happen and some not-so-good things. Yet our souls are wrapped in the blanket of God's eternal Peace and security . . .

APRIL 20

Program: a set of instructions which allow a system to function. Our hearts are programmed to beat; our souls to leap at being loved and in giving love. Let's not let our abusers corrupt our infinite and God-given programming to love ourselves and others.

APRIL 21

We thought that the abuse rendered us useless and helpless. But, when we tell our simple story of survival, an amazing thing happens. We liberate another soul as well as re-liberating our own. Our story is as precious and unique as our own Spirit.

APRIL 22

Our wounded souls are crumpled into a contorted mess. We are healed when we allow the Kind Energy to restore our wrinkled and chaotic spirits. Then we can pass on Love to the next vulnerable person who requires kindness.

APRIL 23

Where are we – stuck in the conflicts, uncertainty and pain of the abuse? Let's take an action towards freedom – and take a nap.

Rest – we need it to continue our personal journey to freedom and our mission to liberating all the Earth from cruelty and selfishness.

APRIL 24

The trees that weather the storm best, bend with the winds of change. Let's not be like the unyielding trees, with willful resistance to help, that stubbornly break. Let's accept help and kindness as well-deserved water to our parched souls.

APRIL 25

Springing up all around us, are signs of hope. With wonder, we observe small miracles of Nature. Even though it may seem that we have a long way to go, our own souls heal every day from the abuse.

APRIL 26

Invading our defenses, the abuse we went through broke our hearts and tortured our very souls. We were shocked, injured, damaged, traumatized and devastated. However, just as deeply as we felt the pain of the abuse, so can we feel joy, healing and Love.

APRIL 27

We have been made so holy and "tenderized" by our sufferings that the abuser's attempts to cause us to hate and seek revenge, will be rendered powerless. Time and God's healing Hands will assure this.

APRIL 28

When the flights of a bird or pastoral scenes move us, we remain still and in awe. We are reminded that God's Universe is unique and unending. We too are unique and unending; we too are a part of God's perfect Plan.

APRIL 29

Whether trees whisper their secrets among the leaves, or devils dance upon my soul, I will remember the healing grace of God's Hand upon my heart. I will offer this insight to a fellow traveler.

APRIL 30

Raining internally, I've tried to hide the pain. God supplies me with encouragement, love and self-esteem. I need no longer to hide my tears or my joy.

MAY 1

I see the sunshine in the sky, reaching far and wide. The gray that loomed for hours or years, is passing, leaving me with a fresh start. I experience Peace from torture and abuse on this sunny, warm, God-given day.

MAY 2

Rendered helpless the abuser now has to face God. "Why have I done this?" They must say (or they may not), still feeling perfectly justified in having tortured another being. Knowing what suffering is, let us not impede God's Lesson.

MAY 3

Struck like Gold being tested, our mettle is good enough. We have survived and now we live to tell how it can be done, through Divine Grace, and our own courage. We mourn for our brothers and sisters who did not survive. Yet know their spirits are pure, forever removed from the agonies of torture and abuse.

MAY 4

Silence and lies are tools of the abuser's trade. Therefore, we must speak up boldly, for ourselves and others. Resistance is *not* futile. Let's join together and shed Divine Light on unspeakable acts of injustice. Blow that whistle – tell the truth, for the truth sets us *all* free!

MAY 5

When I saw the most recent slave freed, I wept with joy for that slave was *me*. Still others wait for salvation from being trafficked and thrown away like so much garbage. Human beings and all creatures seek justice, freedom and Peace. Let's be conduits of each other's deliverance.

MAY 6

We may feel crazy with the pain. Still, we know a greater Sanity exists which orders the universe. It can instantaneously render us sound. Usually, the Divine works slowly, softly, gently if we want Her. She softens our jarring shocks and gently leads us back to sanity and health, wholeness, prosperity and Love.

MAY 7

The abusers try to tell their victims that they run the Universe. The tyrants, unfeeling, run their cruel rituals as if they were gods.

But an unseen Greater Power has Her finger on the button of the True Machinery – the Divine laws of constellations, quarks, and human hearts.

MAY 8

Forgiveness of injustices done to me or others that I witness requires that I admit I have no power over what had happened. The deeds are done, the torture occurred; and I am left holding the results in my heart. It is a devastating flood in which my house was swept away; my security, sense of place and belonging. I am devastated as the wind topples what remains of my belongings. I wonder, where is my God in all this?

And then as I meditate over what happened, I recall that God has allowed me to survive, to nurture another Home within.

MAY 9

I become willing to see the good in anything bad that happens to me. Please God make me capable of this kind of insight; for as the stars are brightest in the depth of darkness, I believe I can find meaning in the midst of cruelty.

MAY 10

Mother's Day is sometimes hard for us, who have no mother; either through death or estrangement. If our mother was one of our abusers, it may be hard to love her at this time, particularly if she has rejected us. Yet she gave birth to us and whether she abandoned us, raised us or partially raised us, we were carried to natural term of our birth. We *are alive* and adults now, responsible for our own lives. Any action that our mothers took to keep us alive, remains, like a golden star in the sky, forever shining and showing us the way. God wanted us to live to carry out loving work for Him and no matter how wayward her actions, our mother helped us get there.

MAY 11

Retribution is *not* the answer, to torture and abuse. There is only the peace of knowing, that we refuse to shame or blame anyone, including ourselves. There is only our responsibility for ourselves as we are *today*. With God's help, we are more compassionate because of what was done to us.

MAY 12

A doe scampers across the field with her fawn. They stand in the tall grasses of Spring living for the fullness of today. We can learn from the doe. God protects us from the harm of revenge and hatred, and returns us safely to loving motives.

MAY 13

Sometimes, I think of the ways I've betrayed my own heart, by repeating over and over in my head, the incidents of abuse; rehearsing over and over what I should have said or should have done. Sometimes it's involuntary due to my Post-Traumatic-Stress-Disorder. Yet for me, forgiveness has gone a long way in reducing the spontaneous repetition of those memories of pain. Now, with forgiveness, I am free to enjoy with enthusiasm what *today* has to offer.

MAY 14

Forgive me, God, as I recall how I have hurt others, and failed to honor their Divinity. I have no right to harm anyone, nor to make them feel worthless. My abuse experiences have taught me that. So let me make up for what wrong I've done, and instead let me help the next traveler to feel Loved.

MAY 15

I remember when everything hurt *so much*. Let me focus on all the ways we all need to be loved. Let me do little things with great love that bring joy and delight to my own and others' eyes.

MAY 16

The abuse taught me that I was worthless. Healing from abuse teaches instead that we are Precious Children of God, carriers of Love and kindness. We are worthy of God's and each other's love.

MAY 17

Pretending to enjoy life, while being preoccupied with the resentments of the past, only prolongs our pain. Often we felt deserving of pain. This is the main legacy of abuse. Getting help, of a professional nature, whether it be through recovery programs, clergy, or psychotherapists is *not* a sign of weakness. While we may feel *very* vulnerable in opening up, professional help can be one route to freeing ourselves from self-hatred and granting us entrance to a better life.

MAY 18

Yesterday's pain is gone; a pale contributor to today. What I choose to do *now* makes all the difference. If I have made mistakes in the past, rather than deny my mistakes, I can look at them. I need not be annihilated by my imperfections. I can take a breath and decide how I can do things better.

MAY 19

No matter how shattered my past was, it can bring meaning and purpose to my life, for it gives me compassion for myself and others who are suffering. Compassion is no small thing . . . . It's a gigantic first step toward a more peaceful, loving world.

MAY 20

Like catching a bus back to Hell – ruminating on the past, and who "did me wrong," makes today's joys and love, extinct.

GRATITUDE for Life's small treasures and blessings opens us up to receive bigger blessings and pleasures. Let's strengthen the muscles of gratitude; then the past won't seem so heartbreaking.

MAY 21

Having gratitude, despite our abuse experiences, will help us to see the glass as "half full," rather than "half empty." When we wonder if things could have been different, either in the earlier discovery and reporting of the abuse or the avoidance of it altogether, we squander the hours that remain for us to be present in the joys of the moment.

MAY 22

We are not "less than." Our first job was to survive the torture and abuse, any way that we could even if it was messy, to do so.

MAY 23

Now is the time to gather our spiritual forces, to grieve our past. It takes great strength to grieve.

A loving God frees us to feel the full spectrum of human emotions. Just as deeply as we feel grief, so too will we feel profound joy.

MAY 24

Tonight I feel the fullness of joy at being alive, at having survived unspeakable horrors. I have escaped – I am free. My life is *my own*, now. I am free to follow the loving Plan of my Maker. Doing so will bring me the greatest joy!

MAY 25

I no longer blame myself for being unable to escape the abuse before I did. My escape came in God's time. I have no regrets. I only feel relief and joy at being alive. As I move forward, how can I respond with compassion for others who suffer, and for myself?

MAY 26

The day of my release from torture and abuse will come soon. I must be patient. With God's help, I will be released from the current abuse situation to a new life of safety and freedom. God and the friends I have not yet met, will be with me – I am not alone.

MAY 27

I watch sunlight slowly warming the landscape. It is a day of Hope. What will I do, today, with my freedom? I will savor the joys of being alive and safe from torture and abuse, at last! This is a *new, unfamiliar*, feeling. But I don't have to latch onto another abusive person, just to get back the old, painful sense of familiarity. I will be courageous and let peaceful feelings sink in, even though they are unfamiliar.

MAY 28

How do I face my guilt that I cannot save everyone from abuse?
I can trust God that some day I will be able to help those still
in captivity.

MAY 29

I will love myself even though it is a challenge. I'll be good to myself and build a healthy, enthusiastic and creative lifestyle, that fills me with joy. My joy will spread to others as a happy contagion, lighting up others' lives, and making them feel warmer and more loved, for my having been here on Earth. My abuse traumas will not block my joy.

MAY 30

I was resourceful in escaping the abuse. Yet I feel remains of the powerlessness I felt while being abused. That I escaped at all was a miracle of God. Now I will call on Divine help, to allow me to assist others to escape their prisons of abuse and torture.

MAY 31

My heart is building a Temple of Peace. I was hurt very badly; but I'm cultivating compassion for myself. I'm choosing to forgive my perpetrators, so I'll have true piece of mind. I am loved by God, and by my chosen family of friends. Let me not forget how blessed I truly am!

JUNE 1

I used to whistle in the wind to keep away my fears, to cope with the terrors of the nights, the days of harm and abuse.

Yet today, I keep silence in my soul because peace has descended on me letting me know in Whose care I belong.

JUNE 2

Happiness is . . . . . helping others to reach peace, and surrender to joy! That is my purpose, now. For *I* have peace, a chance to end darkness, cruelty and fear in the world. We are no longer alone . . . . We are one in God's Divine lap.

JUNE 3

Collectively, we are a power which is beyond all understanding: we have the ability to shape the lives of our brothers and sisters for the better. We are fortunate, for we have already escaped the terrors of the night, when evil was perpetrated on us. Now we act to free others and pray for those in need.

JUNE 4

After the pains of our past sufferings have been lifted, we realize that it was not *we* who were ugly and unacceptable, but it was the ones who were responsible for our pain who are blemished. *They* must bear the responsibility. We pray for them to be released from *their bondage* – their compulsion to commit depraved acts of cruelty. We pray for their release to freedom and Love.

JUNE 5

I approach the sunlight with caution: too much bright light, too much happiness overwhelms me, and I am afraid. After having been in the darkness of being victimized for so long, my eyes and heart must slowly grow accustomed to the safety and warmth of freedom. God understands my hesitance and waits by patiently.

JUNE 6

I feel blank places in my life. God knows what is missing, as I re-associate the emotions I had numbed away, during the traumas, because they were too painful to bear at the time. This process is painful. I must feel the fear, the anger, the sadness, the loneliness, the pain of the abuse, even after it is over. I could not let myself feel the feelings, then. The process gathers to me the pieces of myself that were once missing and I am becoming whole again.

JUNE 7

All the beloved dead who have gone before me to the hereafter assist God and the Angels to help me to be whole and renewed. I answer to God for my efforts to help others to be free; yet I am never alone with the Host of Heaven.

JUNE 8

Rather than make what would seem to be an innocent joke at another's expense, I train myself to seek peace and a sober reflection of that person's Divine worth. Thus, I bring less harm, less cruelty and less violence into the world.

JUNE 9

Beneath the deep grief about being victimized, there is joy. There is a time for mourning and a time for rejoicing. Let me learn to tolerate unfamiliar joy, and to finally embrace it.

JUNE 10

When it's time to close the book on grieving, a certain peace descends. We may feel alone, temporarily, as the grief has its full expression. When we have permitted ourselves to grieve, it is then that serenity can descend and we know we're one with all Creation.

JUNE 11

We may have forgotten that one aspect that gives our lives meaning is the giving and receiving of love from others. Our ability to receive love may have been seriously impaired by abuse, because we do not trust others and we judge ourselves as unworthy of love. Yet love, pure and healing as it is, is our God-given birthright.

JUNE 12

Giving Love is truly listening with the heart as well as the mind. We are interested in how another person feels. We embrace our common "Beingness"– we are not alone.

JUNE 13

If we listen to ourselves and others with no expectation, we find a miracle that connects all experience in gracious understanding.

The abuse had taught us that we had nothing worthwhile to share. We learn through Love that we have everything to share – ourselves; and that we are good enough.

JUNE 14

We contemplate peace, understanding and joy. In this place of meditation we are *not* alone.

Soul murder may have been attempted; yet God revives our drooping spirit and reignites our sense of wonder.

JUNE 15

It may be hard to believe that those who abused us were – innocent, too…even though they chose to use their powers to hurt us and their acts may have seemed directed like a laser on our very souls. What brought them to the extremes of their perverted use of their powers, can only be described as blind desperation, a soul sickness. Our prayers for the abusers may melt the icy exteriors of their hearts. Even though no change may be noticeable from the outside, Love and prayer are *never* wasted.

JUNE 16

"Love is for the weak," declares the abuser. They thought that we were *weak,* because we allowed the abuse to happen. Or, they said we were too "sensitive," and we should just "take it like a man . . .".

Yet Love is most potent in its healing gentleness. It's much easier to slap someone in the face when we're angry, to retaliate and plan all manner of attack. It satisfies our animal desires for revenge.

Love is stronger than hate, because it requires self control, forethought, humility and unselfish consideration of another's viewpoint and well-being, as opposed to giving in to our own self-righteous anger.

JUNE 17

Love is quiet and mighty! Love empowers our beings, and allows us to let go of the past pain and future angst. For Love, only this moment exists. Love renders us real; we see that we are all precious.

JUNE 18

When I felt there was nothing left to live for, it seemed more reasonable, more rational to die; I was a failure, or so I thought. I had not considered all those million little things I've done to express love and consideration for others. Abuse taught me to devalue kindness as weakness.Yet kindness is the only thing that melts the hearts of ice.

JUNE 19

The storms make the trees stronger. Our trials and sufferings make us stronger. We do not give up our quest for meaning. Instead, we know that together with God, we co-create our life's purpose.

JUNE 20

Now is the time to respect each living Being. I respectfully acknowledge myself and others. Abuse obscured how precious we all are, but recovery restores my wonder and reverence for *all* Creation.

JUNE 21

I now experience periods of Peace, wonderment, Love, which the abuse experiences almost completely took away from me. The rage inside me is being healed and hopefully within you, too. A tiny plant pushing its way up through the Earth is like our burgeoning spirits, seeking the sunlight of Joy and Love.

JUNE 22

I like comparing my heart to a lush garden. First, we sow the seed, not really knowing how the plant will grow. The first little leaf opens and we realize: *There is Hope*. If a plant can thrive despite hardship and uncertainty, then so can we. Like the new plant, we require rest, as we grow through the painful feelings of our abusive past. But it's worth the effort to reach a fragrant new life.

JUNE 23

I will cherish today, for that's all I have. Tomorrow is a dream and yesterday a memory. Let me be present in this very moment, and not lose sight of my value. I'm a Precious, unique person, never to be duplicated again – one unique soul, as unique as the stars, the nebulae, the planets, and the tiniest atoms.

JUNE 24

Stars cross the Heavens on their unique flight path. I will live my life in my own unique way. No experience of abuse can belittle the uniqueness of my destiny. We are wonders of God, like rivulets that stream down the mountainside into the mighty river that is God's world, to join at last with all the other unique souls.

JUNE 25

I can explain what has happened to me, either with stubborn resentment, or with gratitude that I've survived, and can choose as a result of my suffering, to have compassion for myself and the entire world.

JUNE 26

When I was being victimized, the pain seemed unending. But I will not give in to hatred and resentment. Instead, I will rely on Someone to bring meaning to my pain, and I will choose Forgiveness, Trust and Love, now.

JUNE 27

As I see the sunrise of a new day, I hope for a time when all Beings will be free of abuse and cruelty. Let's all work together an end to torture and abuse. We can have a new existence built by compassion and deep understanding and reverence for one another.

JUNE 28

Have you had a taste of freedom, yet you are still in an abuse situation? Like a bird learning to fly, you await your opening to leave. Have courage, for once you are free, life will be about so much more than merely surviving. You will be free at last to *thrive*.

JUNE 29

Have pain – will travel – to a not-so-distant land where *abuse is over* and forgiveness lives. Little by little, I am letting go of my need to punish those who hurt me so gravely. My need for revenge is evaporating. I will choose to live in Peace, now.

JUNE 30

When I make a wish upon a dandelion, I bless the seeds that float away. They are like me, free from misuse of power and hurt. The seeds are like the souls who ascend to heaven and leave their tears behind.

JULY 1

Reaching for the stars, while my toes grasp the Earth, I envision a better world, where everyone is free from the abuse, free to just be – and to do all we dream of doing.

JULY 2

Wherever I am, I see Love being manifested. I hold out the hope for all our brothers and sisters who are not yet free of abuse and torture, misuse and debasement, that someday soon they will be free to experience the bliss we now have.

JULY 3

Considering the losses from cruelty and selfishness, let's now, this day, assertively oppose these forces with forgiveness, empathy and compassion. Love will surely melt the hearts of ice that caused our brothers and sisters so much pain. Justice will prevail.

JULY 4

Vengeance is not an option. Though we may feel hatred and anger, we must learn to discharge them safely, so that no one, including ourselves, is hurt. In this way, we break the cycle of abuse through the generations.

JULY 5

Through our experience of great suffering, we learn to act compassionately toward our fellow beings in the Universe. We feel what they feel, and we love them through the pain.

JULY 6

What Mystery lets us live and grow, despite having been tortured and abused? It is the deep Love of God that we can emerge through our suffering, to create a greater purpose.

JULY 7

I believe in a future for myself and my fellow Beings in the cosmos that is kinder, warmer, more loving.When we walk away from cruelty, we create a pathway for both the abused and the abuser to walk side by side together in harmony, repentance and forgiveness.

JULY 8

We cannot grieve in a vacuum; we seek the comfort of open arms and profuse tears, until we cry all the shadows of our loneliness away. Next, we will open our arms to the coming ranks of the sorrowful, until they know for certain that they, too, are Loved.

JULY 9

Recharging our batteries in some contemplative way, through sports or prayer, meditation or song, art, music or dance, we touch the Divine. The Soul murder of torture and abuse was engineered to snuff out our Divine spark but failed to do so. We are Divine "stuff," holy and everlasting. In all of Eternity, not one of us will ever be repeated.

JULY 10

I must respond to my own needs first before I can respond to yours. I must be full to overflowing, first, before I can give to you. The legacy of abuse taught me to "give until it hurts" and to deny my own humanity. Freedom wisely teaches that I must only give out of my Abundance.

JULY 11

We place flowers on the graves of those who have not survived the cruelty of abuse and torture. Though they have died, some of their sweet essence remains. The perpetrators could not take away our brothers' and sisters' Divinity, which lasts forever.

JULY 12

Render me harmless, O God, if I think for a minute of harming another human being. It matters not whether that person is President or homeless beggar, victim or abuser, disturbed or sane. I must show compassion for all . . . .

JULY 13

How can I love my neighbor as myself? – Especially if they have hurt me. First, I will express my outrage, cry out the humiliation, fear, betrayal, grief, pain; and when all has been safely expressed – I am determined to forgive.

JULY 14

In the midst of all turmoil with heart in shock yet again, with pain, disbelief at humans' cruelty to one another, let's remember that God's love melts our nightmares away. He heals hearts, souls, bodies and minds, emotions and intellect, until Peace reigns supreme.

JULY 15

We have been so preoccupied with our pain, that we've missed the beauty of the dawn or the mystery of a flower. The perfume of a delicate flower touches our pain, betrayal, grief and anger. It is ethereal, yet powerful enough to lift our hearts to the Divine so that we hope again.

JULY 16

When things are very bad, let's not lose hope, in God's infinite Love. God encourages us to keep on hoping for one more day, until rescue finally comes.

JULY 17

What can I see through eyes clouded with tears? When we are at "rock bottom," sadness, unbearable pain, unquenching loneliness, blinding rage – this is when our spirits move, learn, and grow. We admit and accept that we are not omnipotent. We realize that we need help, from an all-Loving, all-comforting Divine Power. We seek Her sometimes shakily, haltingly, fearfully. When we find God, peace then descends. We are more than our failures, weaknesses or foibles. – We are Divine spark.

JULY 18

Have you ever wondered what's in the castle of your heart? Can all the rooms be known, or are there so many that new rooms are being discovered daily? Abuse said: "Do not explore who you really are." Though unfamiliar, Divine Providence guides us down new hallways to our Destiny.

JULY 19

Bravest of souls, will you hear me call out to know you better? Our experience with abuse taught us never to reveal our true selves – not to talk or trust, not to feel. However, a new age is dawning which requires more courage, to reveal our true selves, our feelings, dreams and hopes for the future. The Universe supports our revelation, because with it we come closer to doing that most joyful will of God, as our mission, our unique Way of Love.

JULY 20

I raise my eyes to the stars and contemplate the awesome beauty of the Heavens. Empathy for myself and others reveals the awesome beauty of our souls . . . .

JULY 21

In greeting strangers, we find kindred spirits in our common humanity. We all hurt, we bleed, we laugh, we cry – we need Love. We need validation and reassurance, to be held, to be taken seriously, to be loved. – These are what join all regardless of race, religion, customs or the abuse we experienced in the past.

JULY 22

I seek the warmth of the Sun in the vast Heavens. Angels look down and help me. Purification of the mind and spirit from all bitterness is necessary, for me to feel any true happiness – joy I can then pass on to others.

JULY 23

This odyssey through hurt and pain, humiliation and shame, has not been without purpose. Our journey through suffering teaches us compassion for our fellow travelers on the road to Life. Compassion, a most valuable gift, may not be able to be purchased in any other way, than through our own pain. We join with others and now work to end the cycle of abuse.

JULY 24

We imagine what has hurt the abusers so grievously as to cause them to inflict such pain on others. We learn that we were not singled out especially for the abuse: a hurting person lashes out at anyone in the position or role in which we found ourselves.

JULY 25

Abuse of one's power to hurt others, can be difficult to forgive. Betrayal is most painful. It is a spiritual illness that causes this perverted use of power. We can imagine the perpetrator of abuse in a "sick bed," for treatment of their agonizing malady. In our mind's eye, the perpetrator suffers painful symptoms of soul sickness, like the chills, pain, vomiting, fever, bleeding of a physical sickness. We know they suffer gravely. Then we can truly feel compassion, and a desire to help.

JULY 26

I feel the Love of God in every tender living thing. I, too, am a manifestation of the Love of God, no matter how I've been abused, or how broken I am. Let me use my brokenness to help another person to feel at ease, so that they may accept their own Divinity.

JULY 27

Soon a time is coming when all Beings will live free of cruelty and exploitation. That time will come, sooner rather than later, if we but peacefully, yet firmly intervene.

JULY 28

We know that mass rape in the sex trade is taking place. We know that children are cruelly beaten and abused by their parents and caregivers. We know that animals suffer horrific abuse; and that partners suffer both subtle and life threatening abuse from their spouses; we know there is bestial sadism in war. We know from our own experiences of suffering about humanity's cruelty to other beings. What is our hope? The Hope is in our renunciation of violence within our individual selves and the reform of our own spirits. Rather than snap to retaliate, we learn to err on the side of compassion.

JULY 29

Now is the time for me to renounce violence within myself, to eschew all traces of unkindness to any being including myself. If I feel rage and anger, let me learn to express these safely; like the safe discharge of a gun – where no one is hurt. For, these feelings must be felt, and safely expressed – the key word being "safely." I must protect myself and others from the thoughtless, selfish or misdirected expressions of my anger.

JULY 30

Most of us desire the peace and tranquility of a mother's love. We may not have ever been permitted to experience such love, because of loss of mother, through death, illness or through cruelty or neglect. We can remember that God will provide us with mothers throughout our lives; people who care about us. It is really *God's* presence in the form of these people. I am grateful.

JULY 31

Have you ever noticed that when the subject of religion or politics is spoken about, it is really about us – our needs, our wants, our fears, our hopes, our dreams? When we remember every world affair is about someone like me, we recognize our brotherhood and sisterhood.

AUGUST 1

When we recognize that we are all children, that is when we truly grow up. For then, we can forgive our own and others' faults. We can look to peaceful means to meet each other's needs.

AUGUST 2

When people hurt us, let's not hide away and pretend it did not happen. We were taught by our perpetrators to pretend we aren't upset; and to instead allow resentments to secretly fester. This is the way of victimhood. No, let us assertively (not aggressively), state our truth honestly; that we have somehow been disrespected or violated. Whatever the response, at least we have championed ourselves in a peaceful manner.

AUGUST 3

Our spirits, our feelings, our temple-bodies may have been traumatized. We bleed actually or figuratively. Our souls scream out for relief and justice. What form will this justice take? We must tell our truth to the world and seek justice through peaceful means, rather than through retaliation, which only escalates the world's negativity.

AUGUST 4

It may feel uncomfortable and unfamiliar when good things start happening to us; as well as when trustworthy, loving and supportive people start coming into our lives. It may feel extremely disorienting, after being used to nothing but trauma and pain. As adults, we may even have unconsciously sought out individuals who would abuse us, because abuse felt safe in some way – it was familiar. With recovery from trauma, we may realize that the Divine loves us unconditionally, and that in fact, we are fully worthy of all good things.

AUGUST 5

Wanting to protect ourselves from abuse is natural. When we are abused repeatedly, those natural defenses are stripped away, via shaming, terrifying, rageful acts by our perpetrators. As children we learn to associate comfortability with abuse of power and being defenseless victims. When we are recovering, we find our voice, and learn to resist all efforts to shut us down. Our natural defenses are again brought into play, and we no longer tolerate being abused.

AUGUST 6

I felt undeserving of love and good things. Coming to the point where I feel deserving requires me to 1) become aware of how undeserving I actually feel; 2) sit with those feelings and 3) love my inner children and imagine their innocence and deservedness of Love and good things.

AUGUST 7

I now have calm, soothing days, and nights of peace. This came about sometime after being hurt by my abusers. I now know they can no longer hurt me. But, then came the memories, emotional states of terror that I had dared not feel while the abuse was happening. The intensity of the terror and rage rendered me incapable of functioning. And when the PTSD episode was over, I felt *relieved*. I learned to be patient as all the dissociated feelings which were split off at the time of the trauma, have been felt and incorporated. It is then that I will become whole once again. As time goes by and more of my "lost" feelings come back to me – I find far less terror or rage in my life anymore.

AUGUST 8

When we feel pain and shame, sadness, guilt, fear and anger, these are all parts of ourselves. When we *allow* ourselves feel them, though they are unpleasant, we reclaim our wholeness and our right to *feel all of our feelings*, not just the fun ones.

AUGUST 9

Now we are open to the experiences which bring us healing –
even if these lead temporarily, to PTSD episodes... For, we
are healing from the painful feelings and we are learning to
welcome in the positive experiences. We've learned we are
worthy of the process.

AUGUST 10

We are welcoming a time when attempts at our soul murder are healed. We may have to go through terror, rage, sadness and pain, to get to the other side. We regain our own lives, souls, wishes, dreams, destinies, unencumbered any longer by perverted acts of abuse.

AUGUST 11

I remember when it was all I could do to keep on living, one moment at a time. My abuser loomed large, overpowering me and forcing me to their will. I escaped, by God's Grace to a place of no more beatings, psychological torture or abuse. That first night I no longer felt afraid. I was *free*, at last.

AUGUST 12

For those who still suffer, the torment seems endless, and the ability to help oneself seems impossible. Maybe there *is* nothing one can do right now. Continue to pray for your opening, an escape from the terror and madness. So many of us *have* escaped and more will continue to do so. And, the world community will rise up and put a stop to all abuse and torture.

AUGUST 13

If we look at a problem from its narrowest perspective, we see only ourselves. We do not see how others like us may be suffering, nor how we can contribute to a common solution. We see only our own pain and may often feel that our own unworthiness caused the abuse. We have not seen how misuse of power is part of the lower vibratory energy of certain people on Earth. By joining with other survivors, strengthening ourselves and each other with assertiveness training, self defense skills, stronger laws, we can wipe away all abuse.

AUGUST 14

When we find a solution to our own ability to abuse power over other beings, we begin to cure our human weaknesses. All of us are capable of "lording it over" someone else – either through direct abuse or through co-dependency by not allowing another person to take responsibility for their own lives. Overcoming the tendency within ourselves, to abuse power is the first step in healing the world of cruelty and harm.

AUGUST 15

When we neglect ourselves we continue the legacy of abuse that was perpetrated on us. Loving ourselves, even when it is hard to do so, may entail cooking for ourselves, bathing – being fiscally responsible, attending therapy, and meeting our needs for love, kindness, recreation and solitude. These simple acts cut our connection to the legacy of abuse.

AUGUST 16

Reverence towards all life minimizes the possibility of abuse of any life. Now it is time for us to recognize the value of our own lives; our precious, unique, often broken, yet perfect lives. Let's not devalue any being's life, especially not our own.

AUGUST 17

A person without a conscience is our greatest challenge in the fight to end abuse and torture. Yet other people may be so convinced that they themselves are at fault whenever anything, even something small goes wrong. Those lacking conscience need a better standard for themselves to strive for, and those with too much conscience, need to stand up for themselves. In this way we can create a just world.

AUGUST 18

Shouldering the responsibility for ourselves, our needs and our deeds, is half the battle in a world free of abuse and cruelty. Creating laws and raising our children with conscience is the other half. Love demands responsibility and is best achieved when we all work together.

AUGUST 19

After the flow of tears has gone, and our anger and outrage have safely been acknowledged and released, we breathe in the clear air of Love and healing. We become more whole and compassionate towards ourselves and others. We are an evolving world: and while it may take a little time, cruelty and abuse will evaporate from the Earth.

AUGUST 20

What changes have we gone through to arrive at a more peaceful state, after escaping the abuse? Our evolving selves reflect an evolving world; and make us, with our stories of suffering and compassion, Ambassadors of Peace.

AUGUST 21

When we learn to value ourselves as worthy of respect, dignity and love, we lift the dignity of the whole world and chase the abusers out from their hiding places and make them answer for their crimes. In the telling of our truths, is the possibility of redemption.

AUGUST 22

Forgive the abuser? It is their degradation of their own humanity that started them on their abusive paths. Forgiveness offers the possibility of redemption.

AUGUST 23

When we think about our pasts, we may theorize about why the abuse happened. Yet it may not be important to know the whys and wherefores. Instead let us concentrate on how best to recover; realizing that our recovery helps others to recover, too. No experience is wasted when we can share it with a fellow sufferer.

AUGUST 24

When it feels impossible to tell our story one more time, because it brings up all the old pain, we remember the opportunity for healing that the telling can afford us and the world. The new insights that occur to us and to others as they tell *their* stories, will teach us *all* how to live kinder, more Loving lives.

AUGUST 25

We did not cause the abuse, we couldn't control it, and more than likely we could not stop it. We had to find some other way to survive long enough to get away in the hope of a new life.

AUGUST 26

We turn to God with thanks, that our days of being tortured and abused are over. We turn our faces towards the sun, its warming glow refreshing us with hope. Now is the time to live and breathe and hope, even if our future path is uncertain. We are not alone; we will be guided to our most joyful and fully realized path.

AUGUST 27

We may try to forget our memories of pain and abuse. All we want to do is look forward. However, our past is an important part of us, as surely as our promising bright future. Our story can give courage to someone else to tell their story.

AUGUST 28

When will we smile? When all the pain is gone? Tipping the balance in favor of joy, we see our past as a landscape behind us. *It is not our shame.* It is the shameful acts by our perpetrators that must be reckoned with. Being abused does *not* make us to be "less than." We did not cause it, and, having learned compassion, we will not pass on the legacy of abuse.

AUGUST 29

When we were born, we were perfect in every way. Abusive caretakers may have neglected and abused us, causing us to hate our vulnerabilities and ourselves. We were not powerful enough to meet our own needs, nor strong enough to ward off the abuse. Our recovery today, depends upon our ability to recognize our vulnerabilities *then*, and to champion our vulnerable selves *now*.

AUGUST 30

Due to being hurt, we may close ourselves off from receiving love and from doing the things which make us happy. Healing from torture and abuse make us more able to open up and allow the joys which make life worth living.

AUGUST 31

Satisfying our needs for friendship and love is not an easy thing, when abuse has been in the picture. Either we repeat the abuse dynamics with new friends or we feel totally unworthy of love in its purest form. Instead, if we reach to the Source, we find the courage to let go of our feelings of unworthiness, and to embrace Love and happiness in all its forms.

SEPTEMBER 1

Genius is our ability to *survive* adversity; now can we apply that same ingenuity to *thriving*? Little by little, despite our history of being abused, we can get used to good things happening in our lives, like prosperity, health, love and friendship.

SEPTEMBER 2

Now is the time to enjoy our lives, even though we were once victimized. We may not be perfect, our partners may not be perfect; yet if our unions are loving and non-abusive, we are richly blessed, indeed.

SEPTEMBER 3

None of us were ever meant to suffer being tortured or abused.
Nor were we meant to inflict any kind of suffering on others.
To love and be loved – that is the purpose of life.

SEPTEMBER 4

Gumption is the mark of a survivor, as is ingenuity, in times of crisis. Just as much courage and resourcefulness is required for us to thrive. It takes courage to accept the vast change in life circumstances from the hell of being abused to the heaven on Earth that is being free.

SEPTEMBER 5

Serenity is my present current state; ugly memories are my past. I remember both good times *and* pain. Now I lay me down to sleep, I pray for good dreams rather than times to weep.

SEPTEMBER 6

Above the tempo of my aged ache, I long for sweetness as I wake. Is it really true, that I have escaped the persecution of abusers who hurt me? Can I live free, now, to make my own decisions about what is right for my life? Are my rights respected now? Is this the bright dawn on the first day of the rest of my life?

SEPTEMBER 7

"Fear not" means not to dwell on fear and anxiety. When we were being abused, we had enough to fear. Now that many of us are free from the abuse, let us not look for a replacement to the adrenaline highs and lows we experienced while being abused. Addictions to substances or behaviors or to violence can often substitute for those unhealthy adrenaline highs and lows. Let us pray for peace and serenity in the here and now.

SEPTEMBER 8

We can be afraid of our own power. We may be afraid we'll become as domineering and harmful as our abusers. However, we can embrace our own power around safe people and realize that our power can be used for good, our own good and the good of others around us.

SEPTEMBER 9

Surrendering our will to a Higher Power, means giving up our own ideas of what will work in a given situation; in favor of better solutions. Surrendering our fears, to embrace courage, enables us not only to survive but to thrive.

SEPTEMBER 10

Embracing our power benefits us and others. We may have been afraid that we would become like our abusers, who misused their power to hurt us. What is the answer? We all have the capacity to dominate; yet it is our choices for evil or good – our intent to hurt or to help, that determine our capacity to Love.

SEPTEMBER 11

Embracing success after a life of being abused can be difficult. However, we are much more precious, beautiful, amazing and worthwhile than we'd ever dreamed; and we deserve every success in life.

SEPTEMBER 12

In finally being left alone, we may miss the interaction with our abuser. However, it is through our solitude, that we will at last find ourselves, and feel worthy to pursue our own dreams, aspirations and God-given purpose.

SEPTEMBER 13

Congregating with other people, may feel very strange, if our ability to trust has been severely impaired. If we take our time and slowly allow ourselves to feel and to have contact with trustworthy people, we will find that our lives are greatly enriched.

SEPTEMBER 14

In surrendering our will to a Higher Power, we find solace from our loneliness and fears for the future. We find that this is an abundant universe and we can share in it, as worthy sons and daughters of God.

SEPTEMBER 15

We need not project negatively into the future, just because our past lives were very painful. Life *can* and *shall* be good for us and everyone around us, if we but have faith and trust in Divine Providence.

SEPTEMBER 16

We will find, that though we were frequently criticized, emotionally abused and physically and sexually violated, we are more amazing and wonderful than we could have possibly realized. Let us trust in God to help us accept and embrace our worthwhile selves.

SEPTEMBER 17

I am complete: I have painful memories, and yet I hope for the beauty of today. I trust in the warmth and glow of abundant good fortune, filled with people who love me and whom I love, and a God who never abandons me. Today, I trust.

SEPTEMBER 18

I will not be bound to my past painful experiences, but I will trust and have faith that life can and will get better, not just for myself but for all of us, on planet Earth.

SEPTEMBER 19

Self-reliance can go just so far. Soon I realize I must depend upon worthwhile and trustworthy others and upon my Divine Source for all I require. Despite my history of abuse, I am worthy of Love.

SEPTEMBER 20

I call on my God to help me in becoming all I can be. I may have once believed, due to severe abuse and torture, that I was not worthy of Love or anything good. Yet, today, I boldly stand ready to receive God's blessings and other people's love.

SEPTEMBER 21

If we are very, very angry about what was done to us, or how we were neglected, then let us remain still. We must not lose sight of our power, nor must we hurt anyone, including ourselves. Prayer for strength as we champion ourselves, yet prayer for restraint from acting out is the balance we strive for. At some point, the rage *will pass* and we will emerge cleansed and renewed.

SEPTEMBER 22

Our anger over our past will remain with us until it has cleansed us. We hope for a time soon when we can start to enjoy life. Let us champion ourselves and others who have suffered.

SEPTEMBER 23

Rage may seem like our only friend . . . . But stillness of heart, and patience, especially when we feel like "blowing up," is our best ally. I lift up my heart to the Divine as I give my *whole* self to this process of recovery from abuse.

SEPTEMBER 24

Now is the time for all of us to come together, to discard the hateful and cruel tendencies within us, no matter how much others have acted out on us. Now is the time for us to come together to bring lasting peace, forgiveness and Love to the world.

SEPTEMBER 25

Realizing the cost to us of others acting out their rage upon us, we highly prize restraint. Instead we pray for a warming compassion to come over us, to help us to be forgiving and loving.

SEPTEMBER 26

Compassion and love always disarm hate and cruelty. Our world must embrace the virtues of justice, compassion, patience and understanding to root out the hidden cruelty from the shadows and to transmute hatred to Love.

SEPTEMBER 27

Despite our initial rage over being abused, we become compassionate, when we look to see other poor souls who have been victimized. When we try bringing them comfort, we bring comfort to ourselves.

SEPTEMBER 28

As we embrace and love our inner children, we see how precious real children are and the children in the adults all around us. *Then* we can say true compassion has arrived in the world.

SEPTEMBER 29

We've weathered the storms, so that we could survive to see a new day filled with joy, happiness and Love. Survival was the first step to recovering from abuse and violence. Completing the task at hand, we reach out to other survivors to bring comfort and end hatred and violence from all our lives.

SEPTEMBER 30

As survivors of torture and abuse, we band together. We turn shame into pride, silence into empowerment, isolation into community, and victimhood into self-empowerment. With community empowerment, we will bring about an end to all violence and retaliation in the world.

OCTOBER 1

Remembering what it was like to be hurt, we comfort and reassure other victims and survivors, building community. We educate abusers about alternatives to violence, and learn to Love and forgive ourselves and each other.

OCTOBER 2

"Peace on Earth" is our rallying cry, as together we stoke the passion for peace and justice in the world. We work tirelessly to prevent violence from ever occurring again.

OCTOBER 3

Wishing our past did not happen doesn't make the events disappear. We must face our pain, shame, loss and anger over what was done to us. Only then, by being truly honest about how we feel can we fully let go of our suffering. Then we move from being victims, to being survivors to thrivers.

OCTOBER 4

The sun shines during the day to help us to see clearly the events of our lives. It disappears at night to help us peacefully contemplate the events of our day.

When we review the day's events and see ourselves a little richer, a little wiser, a little more productive, we ask how did we come this far? We have survived by the Grace of God.

OCTOBER 5

Peeking down at us through a cloud, is one idea of God. Another is that "still small voice" inside. Let each person define for themselves who or what God is.

OCTOBER 6

It's a risk trusting a Supreme Being. We have doubts and our own plan to do things our own way. Will our lives ever work? We needed help to escape death at the hands of our perpetrators. Now we need help to regain our lives to the fullest. The question is: Will we trust, or won't we?

OCTOBER 7

Relinquishing our role as subservient to others, we see our lives begin anew. The abusers tried to guilt and shame us into denying our true selves. They taught us to co-dependently serve *their* needs and agenda; now we learn to serve God's Plan and our own dreams.

OCTOBER 8

Having survived through all the days and nights of torture, we now gaze upon the horizon. We are free at last and ready to be healed. We are *not* alone – a Higher Mind has restored us; and now we are gratefully at peace.

OCTOBER 9

We may have turned to addictions to substances or self destructive behaviors, to avoid feeling our pain about what was done to us. Now is the time to abandon all self destructive acts, face the original pain and strive for a better life. Recovery from harm done is possible and well worth the effort.

OCTOBER 10

If we have fallen into addictions of any kind, we may ask ourselves, where will we be tomorrow? The choice is ours. Will we still be trapped like our perpetrators imprisoned us; or will we be better off in the future? The Universe will support our choices for health and a good life.

OCTOBER 11

Our experience of having endured much suffering serves to brand us with the indelible mark of compassion; and thus we are much better at helping others to heal from their traumas.

OCTOBER 12

Anger may be one emotion among many that we feel about what was done to us, and what continues to happen to others. However, we must strive to find constructive rather than destructive answers to the violence within ourselves and others, to create a more peaceful, just world.

OCTOBER 13

Vengeance is not the answer to violence, abuse and exploitation. Instead our hunger for peace will make us work harder to heal those who have been harmed; as well as provide deep soul healing for the perpetrators of cruelty.

OCTOBER 14

When we empty ourselves of the bitterness surrounding our abuse, we heal much faster. If we plan revenge, this will only make us sicker; and the painful details of abuse memories will last much longer.

OCTOBER 15

We have the choice to stay bitter about what was done to us, or to grow beyond the limitations of shame and blame. In forgiving the perpetrators, we can forgive ourselves for our own violent desires.

OCTOBER 16

Do we feel sorry for ourselves? Do we project negatively into the future, believing that we are unworthy of anything good, and that we can't accomplish anything worthwhile? Do we stay stuck in bitterness about the past, or do we reach out for help and do what we can to have a better life? Compassion for what we went through is not the same as projecting negatively and giving up trying to be happy. Compassion recognizes that we are vulnerable, as are all beings on Earth.

OCTOBER 17

Grieving for those like us who have been lost to abuse, torture and exploitation, we turn up the level of awareness by the whole world to those still suffering. Grieving is necessary to wash away the pain and strengthen us to free others who are still being tortured.

OCTOBER 18

Many have lost their lives trying to escape torture, oppression and abuse. Others have fortunately escaped. We turn towards each other and God for mutual support in our grief. We resolve to make this a kinder, more loving world for everyone.

OCTOBER 19

Through repeated abuse, our hearts have been "tenderized" into compassion. We turn to others who have been abused and hurt, and offer our comfort and encouragement.

OCTOBER 20

Err on the side of compassion; err on the side of humanity; err on the side of Love and forgiveness, and champion all beings' dignity.

OCTOBER 21

Thanks be to God for allowing us to have made it through alive. Let us forgive ourselves and our perpetrators for human vulnerabilities. Let's strive to forgive so as to put an end to all retaliation and hatred.

OCTOBER 22

Justice means abusers must account for what they have done. Compassion softens hearts, so perpetrators may choose to admit their wrongdoing and ask for forgiveness. When a community does this, it is healed of all shame and blame.

OCTOBER 23

Our painful past only has meaning if I can turn to my neighbor and say: "I love you, let's live in harmony and peace."

OCTOBER 24

Remembering the past, so as not to repeat it is a good strategy. But let us not live in the past, but strive to better ourselves and our communities with the practices of Love and forgiveness.

OCTOBER 25

Kindness towards ourselves and others heals all our wounds from torture, abuse and exploitation. Let's embrace one another in peace, and let's not forget to offer our comfort and compassion.

OCTOBER 26

Reflecting on what we have been through, we find the loss so profound that we have to stop and pause in prayerful remembrance of those who have died, due to torture and abuse. We remember those still struggling to be free. We utter a prayer and move on, knowing that our prayer alone already makes this a better world. Working for justice and peace, makes it even better.

OCTOBER 27

We look towards the sunshine to bring us joy and hope for the future. Remembering how our lives used to be without hope, now we sigh with gratitude for being free, and have the opportunity to tell our stories.

OCTOBER 28

Originally we thought our lives were a waste, with hope that we would not wake up in the morning. And, even though some of us have escaped the clutches of abuse, many of us still feel like dying. We recall that it takes more courage and strength to decide to live each day, despite our pain.

OCTOBER 29

Wondering what our life is going to be like, now that we are suddenly free of abuse, we realize that not everything is going to be "peachy" right away. There may be numerous pieces of our lives to pick up, handle and get help to put back together. It will not be easy, for quite some time. Yet we are not alone. If we choose to believe in a Divine Presence guiding our lives, and go towards God, like a plant moving toward the light, we may find peace and room to grow.

OCTOBER 30

Raging and seeking revenge are not the way. They keep us in the bitterness of our pain, causing us to constantly relive the horrors of being abused. Instead, forgiveness keeps us alive inside and we find more beauty in life.

OCTOBER 31

After prolonged abuse we can find ourselves confusing abuse with being loved – that the abuse was love, our caregiver's or partner's way of loving us. Seeking a good therapist and a supportive community can help greatly to break up this confusion. Then, we realize that love is not meant to hurt, but love is supposed to feel good.

NOVEMBER 1

From our inner child's perspective, the misery of abuse and always being "in trouble" with our caregivers or abusive partners, got confused with feeling secure and loved. We lost our natural feelings of self worth that would alert us that misery is *not* love.

NOVEMBER 2

Building a self worth that tells us when we're being hurt takes the support of a loving community, time and determination. For, we may have lost our tolerance for feeling good. It may be scary to feel loved and at Peace because they're so unfamiliar. Abuse, being familiar, made us feel secure in a strange sort of way.

NOVEMBER 3

Our tolerance for feeling good, feeling loved, living prosperously and healthily, may have been destroyed by our experiences of abuse. Should we want a good and happy life, we have quite a mountain to climb to relearn to accept positive things in our lives and to do so fearlessly.

NOVEMBER 4

Refunding our misery and embracing change, joy and happiness, love and prosperity can take courage for many of us. Each one of us is special, unique and fully worthy and deserving of the blessings God would like to give us. Therefore, slowly and step by step, let's embrace a community of trusted friends – a chosen family to help us to enlarge our lives and feel justifiably grateful.

NOVEMBER 5

Our reluctance to take in and accept positive new things and people's love can be akin to the eating disorder anorexia, a kind of emotional and spiritual anorexia left over from the legacy of abuse. What can be done to alleviate this spiritual anorexia? Clearly Divine intervention is the answer. A loving community is also part of the answer; and a willingness on our part to increase our tolerance for Love and Joy, little by little.

NOVEMBER 6

Enjoying the support of those near and dear to us, whether they be family or friends as a chosen family, we do ourselves good. We nurture that part of ourselves which may have been given very little nourishment, in the days when we were being tortured and abused.

NOVEMBER 7

We pause for reflection at our own worth and value to God. We may not believe we're worth much, but the Divine Face Who sees life from a more objective perspective, can see our worth, and wants to shower us with Love.

NOVEMBER 8

When we are jealous of someone who has more than we do, even though the feeling is unpleasant and pinched, it is a good sign – at least for those of us deprived by abuse. Jealousy – envy is never pleasant, yet it tells us what it is we desire. It gives us something to strive for; the desire being a kind of appetite, for those of us who do not allow in good things; it can awaken our willingness to accept good things and Love into our lives.

NOVEMBER 9

When we realize how we have survived, we respect ourselves as the spark of the Divine that we are. It may not have been pretty, but neither was it wasteful. Every time we acted or controlled ourselves from acting out, was worthwhile, and has helped to ensure our escape.

NOVEMBER 10

When we remember our neighbor who is still suffering, our realization of another's pains, is akin to a prayer We rise up out of ourselves and our lives and reverence the holiness of the next person.

NOVEMBER 11

Even if we went back and forth repeatedly going to and coming from being with the abuser, we need not punish ourselves for our indecision and doubt, love or obsession with that person. Every time we attempted to leave the abuser, we were getting stronger; like a baby eagle testing her wings until she can fly away.

NOVEMBER 12

We remember how we have cried, alone in the night, thinking no one heard us or cared about our pain. But in the silence and misery, Someone hears us.

NOVEMBER 13

Our abuse is impossible to forget. If we have symptoms of Post-Traumatic Stress Disorder, we may relive it each day. But with determination, our pain can be transmuted to help another wounded soul.

NOVEMBER 14

When I think of how long it has taken me to recover, I think of those who have never recovered, who have died at the cruel, thoughtless hands of their abusers. I am grateful that even though I can be triggered by certain events, at least I have a life left to live.

NOVEMBER 15

The tools for survival and recovery have at long last given me a quality of life that I can extend when I offer my hand to another.

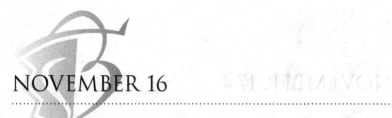

NOVEMBER 16

Have you ever seen the sunset or felt the ocean breeze caressing your cheek at night? Now is the time to embrace all pleasure with gratitude – for they heal us.

NOVEMBER 17

The rose that smells so sweet and the dandelion growing up through a crack in the sidewalk – these are metaphors for our spirits reaching out with courage into the world of beauty and Love.

NOVEMBER 18

Bargaining with God, we lose our way, for we think we are not worthy of Her favor. We feel unworthy of Her unconditional Love, Her being "in our corner," when everything looks bleak or we are less than perfect. However, She sees only perfection in us.

NOVEMBER 19

Now is the time to resolve differences and embrace Love. Let's all be a part of justice and accountability. Then there is Love and peace in our hearts and in the world.

NOVEMBER 20

Our hearts full of Love, we look towards others who are hurting to see what can be done to help them. Our sufferings join with the sufferings of the world and we are one. And just as we are one with each other's sufferings, we can become one in our Joy!

NOVEMBER 21

Balancing ourselves between compassion for ourselves and compassion for others, we see ourselves in a new light: we know there is more to this world than suffering and we offer a smile of recognition, to our brothers and sisters.

NOVEMBER 22

In calmly yet courageously standing up for the rights of others (and ourselves) we create a more just world, a freer world and a safer world. We can create a world where it is safe to be fully ourselves without judgment or shame.

NOVEMBER 23

I recognize the beast in me and the best in me. I recognize the best in you, too. If I control my impulses and listen to you and you to me, we will have Peace.

NOVEMBER 24

Rivers of grief go floating down, deep in our hearts – Let's embrace one another, not criticize . . . .

NOVEMBER 25

I will remember you, as I remember me in our suffering. Even the abuser has pain. Once we are safe from the clutches of the abuser, let us pray for them to be surrounded with a bubble of Bliss and Peace.

NOVEMBER 26

Today I see the sunrise in my heart, its dawning day awakening peace in me and I pray. Today I will rise and go to the dock to welcome incoming refugees from the experience of being abused who are seeking peace and a new life.

NOVEMBER 27

Imagine peace, shifting from pain to Paradise. It may take time – eons till bliss or, with Love – a split-second.

NOVEMBER 28

My heart is filled with tears of joy and peace, embracing all; the peacemakers as well as those bereft of peace – all of us needing Love.

NOVEMBER 29

Consider the exhaustion we felt at being hurt, our emotional skin so paper-thin and delicate, sensitive, wounded. We take to task those who have perpetrated the injuries and we forgive their transgressions, burning away all harm, with Love and Light.

NOVEMBER 30

We seek a stronger reliance on things we feel, but cannot see; such as kindness, warmth and Love. Give to yourself, and to your brothers and sisters.

DECEMBER 1

Where will our world be if we do not participate? Abuse experiences may have taught us to hide . . . Yet what state will our world be in, if we do?

DECEMBER 2

Howlings of pain in our soul draw the mercy of God, Who hears our pain and seeks to comfort us. Would that we would listen to the cries of others, to bring about their peace and recovery.

DECEMBER 3

Hatchlings cry for their Mama – we cry for Peace and for God.

DECEMBER 4

. . . .

Though we may feel very vulnerable, like flowers in spring, let's open our hearts. Closing our hearts only brings more pain and misery into the world.

DECEMBER 5

Abuse shuts us down, as it shuts down the abuser's heart. Contemplate the beating of our hearts, and the pulse of our Life Force, as a way for all, through to peace and joy.

DECEMBER 6

The "sky's the limit." We can do impossible, unfathomable acts of kindness, wandering still into that realm which makes our love everlasting . . . .

DECEMBER 7

Artists teach us the way. We are all artists of Love, offering comfort to the downtrodden, peace to the bewildered, encouragement to the troubled, and Love to the grieving.

DECEMBER 8

Time is passing – won't you give Love to yourself, then to those who are in need of comfort, today?

DECEMBER 9

Our health and/or physical appearance may have been seriously damaged as a result of the abuse. Now is the time to ask for help from experts knowledgeable in the fields of healing and medicine; feeling all the time that we are fully worthy of such loving attention. Let's not skimp on health.

DECEMBER 10

Our abuse experiences may have caused us to suffer from Post-Traumatic Stress Disorder, severe anxiety and dark depression. We ask the Divine energies to give us the courage and openness to reach out and accept effective help. We are no less than a spark of the Divine, and as such are so very worthy of recovery from these painful experiences.

DECEMBER 11

Our finances may have taken a "nosedive" as a result of being abused. Whether we lost the means of survival after a divorce or became an underearner and/or debtor/compulsive spender, after childhood neglect and/or abuse, or are now homeless. God will help us if we ask for help. We will take tiny, baby steps to overcome our deprivations. We deserve no less.

DECEMBER 12

If our depression and rage get all mixed up with terror about the future, we can sit still . . . And *know* in the quietness of our inner spirit, that God loves us. He is *always* in our corner, never judging, always encouraging, as we gradually heal from our abuse experiences.

DECEMBER 13

All Creation is heading towards hope, peace, prosperity, and Love; even if it looks like certain people are slipping behind or doing an about-face. A turn in the right direction can happen at any moment for any of us; and our love and openness toward one another can help to facilitate this.

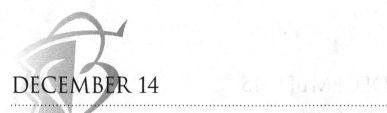

DECEMBER 14

Forever young, our hearts and spirits seek the peace we had perhaps never experienced before. We are fully entitled to its brisk passion, its balmy breezes, its security, surrender, serenity. No matter what we have done or have before experienced we deserve the comforting Love of God.

DECEMBER 15

Thank you, God, for Your Protection – from further harm. I am at Peace, longing for . . . Joy! I deserve Joy and so does all of Creation.

DECEMBER 16

God's help is sacred. Texts of all faiths and of atheism, agnosticism teach me well. I thank the Divine for helping me to survive abuse experiences then; and to thrive in peace, now.

DECEMBER 17

Efforts at excavating long-buried feelings about the abuse are well-worthwhile; to clear them and promote healing and forgiveness. However, let's not allow the abuse experiences to become an excuse for morbid preoccupation with the past, lest we miss the joyful moments of today.

DECEMBER 18

Let not our lives be the constant re-living of our past woes. Rest and know that God is Love.

DECEMBER 19

I'd prefer to remember to smell the lilies and the hyacinths, than to recall the pain of the past. May you easily find your flowers of Deliverance.

DECEMBER 20

God of our understanding comforts us like we are little babies, because to Her, that's what we are – cute, adorable, perfect and full of promise.

DECEMBER 21

Ephemeral the moments of bliss may seem to be; yet they indelibly write in our hearts of the compassionate Love of the Creator.

DECEMBER 22

Beautiful prayers fill our spirits to the brim and give us strength of spirit to try once again to improve ourselves and the world.

DECEMBER 23

This morning, I saw the sunrise. Now, I see the sunset. My life may feel challenging, but though I have suffered, I have begun the path of recovery from torture and abuse.

DECEMBER 24

Cowering no more, we stand straight-backed and duly proud, breathing in the sweet essence of God's Love tickling our spirits with happiness and joy!

DECEMBER 25

If we take the time, many of the feelings which used to trouble us, fade. We distance ourselves from their repetition. If you have a cloud of pain you cannot overcome, tell a fellow; whisper or shout, cry or scream; you are one with the Divine.

DECEMBER 26

If you fear a self-fulfilling prophecy, abuse experiences no matter how depraved, need *not* define us. It is we, in concert with the Divine, who determines what the outcome of our lives will be.

DECEMBER 27

Throw your hearts open: for when we find peace for ourselves and others, we will not let go of it for any treasure in the world.

DECEMBER 28

I cooperate fully with the Lord; His name do I praise; no matter the language or religion or concept – all are blessed. For His deliverance of me, I praise Him, with joy and relief and hope for the future.

DECEMBER 29

Now we must direct our thoughts to the deliverance of this world in its rebirth. Each of us plays a part; and all of us have suffered. Not one among us can remain idle – for we are *all* needed in the world's healing.

DECEMBER 30

I cry no more . . . . My wounds are healed, and so may yours be.

DECEMBER 31

At last . . . our hearts are free. Let us remember all that we have been through, both positive and negative. Let us work together to bring about health and hope, joy and Love to God's wondrous world.

Printed in the United States
By Bookmasters